FAITH AND HEALTH DEVOTIONAL SERIES

REBUILD YOUR TEMPLE
GOD'S WAY®

BOOK 2: RENEW YOUR SOUL

A 10-DAY JOURNEY TO EMOTIONAL
HEALTH AND MINDSET RENEWAL

STEPHANIE L. FRANKLIN-SUBER

Dedication

To my cherished husband, **Berchard V. Suber**, and my son, **Michael Franklin Suber**—thank you for your steadfast love, prayers, and strength through every season of my restoration and renewal.

You have been shining reflections of the faithfulness and compassion of our Lord and Savior, Jesus Christ.

To **Reverend Anna Grant-Borden** and to the members of **Mount Airy Presbyterian Church**, past, present, and future.

To every woman carrying the invisible wounds of emotional or mental pain and anguish—may you find comfort, hope, and renewal in our Shepherd who restores the soul.

With immeasurable gratitude to my **Lord and Savior, Jesus Christ**, who continues to heal the brokenhearted and bind up every wound with His unfailing love.

May You be glorified.

Blessed by the support of Cathy Morenzie, Preston Squire, and Jennifer Eastmond, and by the gifted work of Alec Gerhart and Rachel Aponte.

Foreword

Do you not know that your body is a temple of the Holy Spirit who is within you, whom you have from God, and that you are not your own? You were bought with a price [you were actually purchased with the precious blood of Jesus and made His own]. So then, honor and glorify God with your body.
(1 Corinthians 6:19–20 AMP)

Our bodies are sacred edifices, masterfully created by God for His glory and for worship. In Psalm 19:1, King David declares, *"The heavens declare the glory of God; the skies proclaim the work of his hands."* Just as the heavens reflect the majesty of God, so do we — His beloved creation. We are the workmanship of His hands, *"fearfully and wonderfully made."*

Yet as we journey through life, the demands placed on our bodies — some self-imposed and others thrust upon us by circumstances, people, or illness — can leave us depleted, wounded, or disconnected from the God who created us. In these moments of weariness and brokenness, we stand in need of **restoration**, **renewal**, and **realignment** with our Creator.

In this beautifully architected and God-inspired devotional collection, Stephanie Franklin-Suber gently but powerfully guides you through a sacred journey to restore your body, renew your soul, and realign your spirit.

Stephanie has walked this very path — from brokenness into wholeness through the transformative power of God's Word. God miraculously healed and delivered her from cancer, from years of chronic illness, and most recently from cardiac arrest. In each chapter of her testimony, God revealed to her the sacredness of her temple and showed her that, through faith in Jesus Christ, through Scripture, and by the work of the Holy Spirit, her temple could be rebuilt — God's way. Today, God has called Stephanie to help others rebuild their temples: body, soul, and spirit.

It is with joy and deep gratitude that I introduce you to this ***Rebuild Your Temple, God's Way® Signature Faith and Health Collection***, which includes the three-book *10-Day Devotional Series* (*Restore Your Body*, *Renew Your Soul*, and *Realign Your Spirit*) and the two-book *30-Day Devotional Series* (the *30-Day Devotional* and the companion *Bible Study Workbook*).

As you embark on this sacred journey, do so with **anticipation** and **expectation**. Allow the Word of God to minister to your soul through Scripture and Reflection. Worship God with your body through the daily Temple

Practice. Receive God's healing and restoration by engaging the Health Coaching Tips. And experience spiritual alignment as your spirit connects with the Spirit of God through prayer and journaling in the *Rebuild Your Temple, God's Way® Journal.*

It is my honor and delight to invite you to experience this transformational journey.

Come, and Rebuild Your Temple, God's Way®.

Yours in Christ,
Rev. Anna L. Grant-Borden
Senior Pastor, Mt. Airy Presbyterian Church
Philadelphia, Pennsylvania

Table of Contents

Daily Devotionals
Each day includes Scripture, Reflection, Temple Practice, Health Coaching Tip, Prayer, Journal Prompt, and Affirmation.

You are encouraged to use the Rebuild Your Temple, God's Way® Journal or your own personal journal to capture your prayers, insights, and reflections each day.

Author's Introduction

Your soul—your mind, will, and emotions—is the *Inner Court* of your Triune Human Temple™ (Body–Soul–Spirit).

It is where your thoughts take shape, your emotions rise, and your decisions are made. In the Holy Temple of Jerusalem, the *Inner Court* was a place of consecration—a sacred space between the *Outer Court* of worship and sacrifice and the *Holy of Holies* where God's presence dwelled. In the same way, your soul stands between your body and your spirit, influencing both.

In *Book 1 – Restore Your Body*, we began your Triune Temple Journey™ by rebuilding your *Outer Court*—the visible, physical part of your health journey. Now, in *Book 2 – Renew Your Soul*, we enter the *Inner Court* of your Triune Human Temple™, where emotional healing and renewal of your mind take place. Here, God the Son invites you to lay down fear, worry, doubt, and grief so His peace can reign within.

This devotional is for anyone who has felt the heaviness of emotional exhaustion, trauma, or turmoil. The pages that follow were born from my own journey of rebuilding my temple, God's way. Through cancer, chronic illness, and even cardiac arrest, my soul was devastated again and again—but each time, Jesus Christ faithfully healed and restored it. What He did for me; He can do for you. When your thoughts whirl in tornadoes of fear and anxiety or your heart breaks and aches with despair, discouragement and sorrow, our Savior, as the Living Word, offers renewal.

Just as Jesus calmed the stormy sea, He also speaks peace to the storms in our hearts and minds. He can quiet your mind, heal your emotions, and restore your hope.

Over the next ten days, you will delve into the process of rebuilding your soul—one that replaces fear with faith, anxiety with peace, guilt with grace, and sorrow with joy.

Each day offers:

- **Scripture** to anchor your thoughts in the truth of the Living Word,
- **Reflection** to acknowledge and ponder any brokenness in your heart,
- **Temple Practice** to help you apply what you have learned,
- **Health Coaching Tip** for ways to promote emotional wellness and mindset renewal,

- **Prayer** to surrender and rest in the healing presence of the Prince of Peace,

- **Journal Prompt** to reflect and process your thoughts and feelings, and

- **Affirmation** to carry renewed calm and peace into your day.

Toxic thoughts and emotions are not enemies to suppress but invitations to cultivate a deeper connection with God, the Son. When doubts fill your mind and your emotions are in turmoil, He comforts you and gives renewed hope and joy (Psalm 94:19 NIV).

May these ten days help you experience His healing presence as you rebuild your inner court. Where there is peace in Christ, health and wholeness can take root.

God the Son invites you to go deeper in this journey and renew your soul—His way.

DAY 1 – GUARD YOUR HEART

Scripture
Above all else, guard your heart, for everything you do flows from it.
(Proverbs 4:23 NIV)

Reflection
The heart, in Scripture, represents your whole inner life—your thoughts, feelings, and will. Solomon's command to "guard your heart" is not about building walls but about cultivating awareness. Your heart is sacred ground where God the Son plants truth, but it can also become cluttered by fear, doubt, and distraction.

Guarding your heart means watching what influences your emotions and thoughts. It means choosing what to dwell on, who to trust, and what to release. When you bring every feeling—joy, worry, or pain—before the Son, you invite His peace to protect you. The more you surrender your emotions to Him, the more your heart becomes a place where His love freely flows.

Temple Practice
Pause today and ask, "What has been shaping my emotions lately—the truth of the Living Word or the world's noise?" Offer one burden to Him in prayer.

Health Coaching Tip
Limit emotional overload. Step away from social media or news for a set time each day. Quiet space nurtures emotional clarity.

Prayer
Lord Jesus,
Help me guard my heart with Your wisdom. Protect my thoughts and emotions so Your peace can flow freely within me.
In Your name, I pray, Amen.

Journal Prompt
What does your heart need protection from today, and how can you guard it through prayer and boundaries?

Affirmation
I guard the sacred ground of my heart with the love of Christ. Everything I do flows from it.

DAY 2 – RENEW YOUR MIND

Scripture
Do not conform to the pattern of this world, but be transformed by the renewing of your mind.
(Romans 12:2 NIV)

Reflection
Paul reminds us that transformation begins in the mind. The world trains you to react with fear, comparison, and self-criticism, but Christ calls you to think differently. Renewal happens when you invite the Living Word to reshape your thoughts and replace lies with truth.

Your mind can be a battlefield, but it can also become a sanctuary. Every time you choose gratitude over grumbling or faith over fear, you strengthen new pathways of peace. Meditating on the Word literally re-patterns your brain, restoring your capacity for joy and resilience.

Healing the soul begins with this surrender: "Lord, change how I think so I can live as You see me."

Temple Practice
Write down one negative thought you have been repeating. Cross it out and replace it with a promise from Scripture.

Health Coaching Tip
Feed your mind as carefully as your body. Start or end each day with uplifting music, Scripture reading, or journaling.

Prayer
Lord Jesus,
Please renew my mind with Your truth. Transform my thoughts so they reflect Your mind of peace and power.
In Your name, I pray, Amen.

Journal Prompt
What thought patterns need to change for your mind to align with the truth of the Living Word?

Affirmation
I renew my mind daily by the truth of the Living Word.

 **DAY 3 – LAY IT DOWN**

Scripture
Cast your cares on the Lord and He will sustain you; He will never let the righteous be shaken.
(Psalm 55:22 NIV)

Reflection
David wrote this psalm in a season of betrayal and emotional pain. His words remind us that God, the Son, not only hears our cries—He carries them. To "cast" your cares is to throw them onto His shoulders, trusting His strength to sustain what yours cannot. Emotional burdens—fear, guilt, grief, or disappointment—were never meant to be permanent cargo.

When you hold onto pain, it begins to hold onto you. But when you lay it down before the Lord, you make space for peace to enter. Jesus Christ never promised a life without sorrow, but He did promise His sustaining presence in every storm. Lay down your worries, your regrets, and your what-ifs.

His hands are strong enough to hold them—and gentle enough to heal them.

Temple Practice
Find a quiet space. Write your heaviest concern on paper, then fold it and pray, "Lord, I cast this care on You."

Health Coaching Tip
Chronic stress tightens muscles and drains energy. Stretch slowly while breathing deeply, releasing both physical and emotional tension.

Prayer
Lord Jesus,
I lay down my cares before You. Sustain me with Your strength and fill my soul with Your peace.
In Your name, I pray, Amen.

Journal Prompt
What burden have you been carrying alone that you can entrust to Jesus today?

Affirmation
I cast my cares on the Lord. He sustains me with unfailing peace.

DAY 4 – OVERCOME YOUR FEAR

Scripture
So do not fear, for I am with you; do not be dismayed, for I am your God. I will strengthen you and help you; I will uphold you with my righteous right hand. (Isaiah 41:10 NIV)

Reflection
Fear is a natural response—but left unchecked, it becomes a barrier to peace. Jesus Christ never condemns you for feeling fear; instead, He invites you to transform it into trust. Each "Do not fear" in Scripture is paired with a reason: "for I am with you." The presence of God the Son, is the antidote to fear.

Sometimes fear rises from real wounds or trauma. The limbic system—the body's alarm center—remembers pain and keeps you on high alert. Yet even here, God the Son speaks calm into chaos. As you breathe deeply and speak His promises, you train both your brain and your spirit to rest in His safety. Perfect love really does cast out fear.

Temple Practice
Pause and whisper, "Jesus, You are with me," when fear surfaces. Visualize His hand steadying your heart.

Health Coaching Tip
Ground yourself in the present moment. Feel your feet on the floor, take three slow breaths, and focus on one truth: "I am safe in Christ's care."

Prayer
Savior,
Thank You that Your presence drives out fear. Calm my anxious heart and fill me with Your perfect peace.
In Your name, I pray, Amen.

Journal Prompt
What fear has been keeping you from peace, and how can you invite Jesus into it today?

Affirmation
I will not fear, for Jesus is with me—strengthening and upholding me.

 DAY 5 – CHOOSE PEACE

Scripture
Do not be anxious about anything, but in every situation, by prayer and peti-tion, with thanksgiving, present your requests to God. And the peace of God, which transcends all understanding, will guard your hearts and your minds in Christ Jesus.
(Philippians 4:6–7 NIV)

Reflection
Anxiety is what happens when the soul forgets that Christ Jesus is near. Paul's words are not a command to suppress worry but an invitation to redirect it—to turn anxiety into prayer. When you express your concerns to God, the Son, with gratitude, you exchange chaos for calm.

Peace is not the absence of trouble; it is the presence of Christ within it. Like a guard at the city gate, His peace surrounds your heart and mind, protecting you from fear's return. Each time you choose prayer over panic, you strengthen your trust that He truly is in control.

Temple Practice
Pause and say, "Lord, I give this to You," when anxiety arises. Then, name three things you are grateful for in this moment.

Health Coaching Tip
Establish a "peace ritual." Brew tea, light a candle, or play worship music during prayer to calm your heart and mind.

Prayer
Redeemer,
I am grateful that Your peace guards my heart and mind. Teach me to turn every worry into prayer and worship.
In Your name, I pray, Amen.

Journal Prompt
How does gratitude shift your thoughts and emotions when you feel anx-ious?

Affirmation
I guard my heart and mind in the peace of Christ Jesus.

DAY 6 – REST IN HIS GRACE

Scripture

He does not treat us as our sins deserve or repay us according to our iniquities. For as high as the heavens are above the earth, so great is His love for those who fear Him; as far as the east is from the west, so far has He removed our transgressions from us.
(Psalm 103:10–12 NIV)

Reflection

Shame is one of the heaviest emotions the soul can carry. It whispers, "You are still defined by what you did." But God's grace answers, "You are defined by what My Son has done." David's psalm reminds us that divine forgiveness is not partial—it is complete. The blood of the Lamb removes guilt thoroughly—east and west can never meet again.

When you rehearse regret, you reopen wounds Christ already healed. Resting in grace means believing His mercy outweighs your mistakes. Let His compassion quiet the voice of condemnation until only love remains.

Temple Practice

Visualize laying your regrets at the foot of the cross. As you breathe out, whisper, "I release this to Your grace."

Health Coaching Tip

Self-compassion supports a healthy mind. When guilt arises, practice slow, diaphragmatic breathing to calm your nervous system and remind yourself: "I am forgiven and loved."

Prayer

Redeemer,
Thank You for Your mercy that covers all my failures. Teach me to rest—not strive—in Your grace.
In Your name, I pray, Amen.

Journal Prompt

What past mistake or regret is God inviting you to release into His grace?

Affirmation

I rest in the unchanging grace of Christ. His blood has washed away my guilt and shame.

DAY 7 – REFRAME THE STORM

Scripture
Consider it pure joy, my brothers and sisters, whenever you face trials of many kinds, because you know that the testing of your faith produces perseverance. Let perseverance finish its work so that you may be mature and complete, not lacking anything.
(James 1:2–4 NIV)

Reflection
Life's storms can feel like punishment, yet James reveals they are invitations to growth. Trials expose what is fragile so Jesus can strengthen what is lasting. Reframing a storm does not deny pain; it recognizes purpose.

When you view difficulty through faith's lens, hope begins to surface. Each challenge can develop patience, empathy, and endurance—the spiritual muscles of maturity. Even emotional storms—grief, disappointment, anxiety—become classrooms where the grace of Christ teaches trust. The same wind that bends the tree also deepens its roots.

Temple Practice
Recall one current challenge. Ask Jesus to reveal your weakness and what He is trying to teach you through the trial.

Health Coaching Tip
Stress reframed as "growth energy" changes the body's chemistry. During tense moments, repeat, "This is hard, but it is helping me grow," to shift from panic to purpose.

Prayer
Wonderful Counselor,
Help me see my trials through Your eyes. Strengthen my faith until endurance finishes its good work.
In Your name, I pray, Amen.

Journal Prompt
How might your present storm be shaping Christlike character within you?

Affirmation
I have deep roots of faith in Christ. My resilience is strengthened by every storm.

DAY 8 – HEAL YOUR BROKEN HEART

Scripture
He heals the brokenhearted and binds up their wounds.
(Psalm 147:3 NIV)

Reflection
Grief changes you; it does not have to destroy you. Jesus is always with you. He never rushes your sorrow—He sits with you in it. The Hebrew image of this verse is intimate: God, the Son, personally binds the torn places of the heart like a skilled physician. Every tear invites His tender presence.

Emotional healing takes time and trust. When pain resurfaces, let it become prayer rather than isolation. God's comfort is not abstract—it comes through His Son, His Word, and often through compassionate people. In His hands, your heartbreak becomes holy ground where new compassion grows.

Temple Practice
Write a letter to Jesus about your loss or disappointment. End it with gratitude for His presence in your healing

Health Coaching Tip
Crying is the body's cleansing mechanism. Welcome tears—they release stress hormones and promote calm. Pair tears with hydration and rest.

Prayer
Healer of Hearts,
By Your stripes, I am healed. Thank You for binding my wounds. Hold me close as You turn my pain into purpose.
In Your name, I pray, Amen.

Journal Prompt
Where do you still feel broken, and how has Christ already begun to mend you?

Affirmation
Jesus heals my broken heart and restores joy to my soul.

 # DAY 9 – CULTIVATE JOY

Scripture
Do not grieve, for the joy of the Lord is your strength.
(Nehemiah 8:10 NIV)

Reflection
Joy is not the denial of pain but the discovery of God's presence within it. When the Israelites heard God's law after exile, they wept—but Nehemiah reminded them that celebration, not shame, was their strength. Gratitude opens the door to that same holy joy today.

Each act of thanksgiving—no matter how small—shifts your focus from loss to abundance. Joy does not always shout; sometimes it whispers through sunlight, laughter, or the quiet assurance that God is still good. He gave you His only Son. As you cultivate gratitude, you till the soil of your soul for joy to take root and grow strong.

Temple Practice
List five things—simple or profound—for which you are thankful. Read them aloud as praise.

Health Coaching Tip
Daily gratitude journaling lowers stress and improves sleep. Before bed, record three blessings to train your brain toward positivity.

Prayer
Lord Jesus,
Plant deep joy in my heart. Let gratitude be the song that strengthens me each day.
In Your name, I pray, Amen.

Journal Prompt
How has gratitude changed your emotional outlook recently?

Affirmation
I am grateful for the goodness of Christ, and the joy of the Lord is my strength.

DAY 10 – WALK IN FREEDOM

Scripture
So if the Son sets you free, you will be free indeed.
(John 8:36 NIV)

Reflection
Freedom is more than the absence of bondage—it is the presence of peace. When Jesus spoke these words, He offered liberation not only from sin but from fear, guilt, and every lie that imprisons the mind. Emotional freedom begins when you believe His truth over your trauma.

God, the Son, does not erase your story; He redeems it. The memories that once triggered pain can become testimonies of grace. Walking in freedom means choosing faith daily. It means releasing what no longer defines you and embracing the identity Christ secured for you. You are no longer captive to the past; you are a temple filled with His light.

Temple Practice
Take a short walk outdoors. With each step, thank Jesus for one area of freedom He has given you.

Health Coaching Tip
Movement reinforces empowerment. A brisk 10-minute walk boosts mood and confidence—physical reminders of inner liberty.

Prayer
Lamb of God,
Thank You for setting me free. Help me live each day in Your peace and the confidence of Your truth.
In Your name, I pray, Amen.

Journal Prompt
Where have you seen evidence of Christ's freedom in your emotional life?

Affirmation
I walk in peace, confidence, and joy. The Son has set me free.

Closing Prayer – Renew Your Soul

Lord Jesus,

Thank You for leading me through this journey of soul renewal. You have quieted my anxious thoughts, healed my wounds, and filled the broken places of my heart with peace.

As I continue to guard my heart and renew my mind, teach me to live from a place of trust rather than fear, gratitude rather than worry, and grace rather than guilt.

May You, as the Living Word, continue to transform my thoughts, reshape my emotions, and restore my will to align with Yours. Let my soul be a sanctuary where Your peace reigns.

Thank You for the comfort that calms my storms, the joy that strengthens me, and the truth that sets me free. Renew my soul daily with Your presence, and let my life reflect the beauty of Your renewal.

In Your name, I pray, Amen.

Continue Your Triune Temple Journey™

Congratulations!

You have completed *Book 2 – Renew Your Soul: A 10-Day Journey to Emotional Health and Mindset Renewal* in the *Rebuild Your Temple, God's Way®* *Faith and Health 10-Day Devotional Series.*

During this stage of your Triune Temple Journey™, you have learned to guard your heart, renew your mind, and bring every emotion—fear, grief, doubt, and joy—into the healing presence of Jesus Christ.

Your soul, once weary and burdened, now rests in His peace.

But this is not the end—it is the middle—the inner court of your temple renewal.

From here, you are ready to continue your Triune Temple Journey™ and enter deeper fellowship with God in:

💛 *Book 3 – Realign Your Spirit: A 10-Day Journey to Spiritual Health and Wholeness*

There, you will learn to encounter the Holy Spirit, abide in His presence, and align your spirit with His will.

Visit www.rebuildyourtemplegodsway.com to explore transformational Christian health coaching programs and resources designed to help you reclaim and maintain a life of health and wholeness—body, soul, and spirit—God's way.

Restore Your Body. Renew Your Soul. Realign Your Spirit.™

www.ingramcontent.com/pod-product-compliance
Lightning Source LLC
Chambersburg PA
CBHW040906120626
46551CB00006B/670